WE BOTH READ®

Jason and Bobo
Parent's Introduction

We Both Read books have been developed by reading specialists to invite parents and children to interact as they read together. This particular book is designed for a parent or adult to read the entire book to a child. However, throughout the book the child is invited to actively participate by looking at the pictures and responding to questions.

The book follows Jason and his dog, Bobo, as they spend a delightful day walking around town. However, Jason and Bobo need a little help along the way. Your child can help Jason and Bobo by answering questions throughout the book. After reading a page, you can look at the picture with your child and discuss possible answers to help Jason.

Discussing and answering these questions is not only fun—it will also help your child develop skills that will benefit her in school! The book is like a simple and enjoyable game that you can play together. At the same time, your child will be practicing skills in many areas including reasoning, counting, telling time, and pattern recognition.

See if your child can answer the questions before turning the page to see the solutions. When your child answers one of the questions, consider asking what in the picture made him think of that answer. When needed, you can help your child

think about the questions and point out clues in the pictures to help her think of an appropriate solution.

Depending on your child, it may be helpful to read only a part of the book at a time. It may also be helpful to read this book more than once with your child. In a second reading, consider making up some of your own questions or discuss other things that are happening in the scenes. Remember to praise your child's efforts and keep the interaction fun.

Try to keep these tips in mind, but don't worry about doing everything right. Simply sharing this book with your child will help him to develop skills that will be important in school as well as provide an enjoyable experience for both of you.

Jason and Bobo

A We Both Read® Book
Level PK–K

Text Copyright © 2019 by Sindy Mckay
Illustrations Copyright © 2019 by Meredith Johnson
Reading Consultant: Bruce Johnson, M.Ed.

Published by
Treasure Bay, Inc.
P.O. Box 119
Novato, CA 94948 USA

Printed in Malaysia

Library of Congress Catalog Card Number: 2018952105

ISBN: 978-1-60115-354-8

Visit us online at
TreasureBayBooks.com

PR-11-18

WE BOTH READ®

Jason and Bobo

By Sindy McKay

Illustrated by Meredith Johnson

TREASURE BAY

The summer sun was shining through Jason's window when he woke up. It looks like it's going to be hot out today! What clothes do you think Jason should wear?

1

Shorts and a T-shirt are just the thing for hot weather. Now he needs to put something on his feet.

Hmm . . . it looks like Jason's socks and shoes got all mixed up. Can you help him find a pair of socks and a pair of shoes that match?

The striped socks are a perfect match! So are the red sneakers!

Now Jason can go and have breakfast.

Jason is happy to see pancakes on the table, but he sees some things that don't belong there. What do you think doesn't belong on a breakfast table? Where might be a better place for those things?

The hammer, wrench, and screwdriver don't belong on the table. A better place for them might be in a toolbox.

The tools remind Jason of the fence they're putting up at the park. He and Bobo go to check it out.

Jason is curious to know how many wooden boards it took to build this fence. Can you help Jason count them?

Jason counted nine wooden boards in this fence.
Bobo is proud of him!

Jason notices that the wooden boards have been painted in a certain pattern. Do you see the pattern? Following the pattern, what color do you think the next board should be?

Did you figure it out? The pattern is red, blue, green, red, blue, green, red, blue . . . GREEN.

Uh-oh. Bobo has spotted a squirrel. Off she goes!

The squirrel is going up a tree. Bobo wants the squirrel to do just the opposite! What is the opposite of *up*?

The opposite of *up* is *down*. Do you know some other "opposite" words?

Jason spots some kids playing baseball. When he joins them, he is puzzled by their equipment. Something doesn't belong. What item doesn't belong?

The fire hose doesn't belong at a baseball game.
It belongs on a fire truck. Jason volunteers to bring
it to the firefighters.

On the way to the fire station, Jason and Bobo stop for lunch. Jason wants two hot dogs and Bobo wants one. How many total hot dogs do they need to buy?

Three hot dogs are just what they need! Two for Jason and one for Bobo. Yummy!

Now it's on to the fire station!

Jason and Bobo arrive to find a cat is stuck in the tree outside the station. The firefighters want to get the cat down, but they can't figure out the right order to do it in. Can you help? What do you think is the correct order for these pictures?

That looks right. Now the firefighters can get the cat down, safe and sound.

Jason is ready to leave now, but he can't find Bobo. Do you see her? Can you describe to Jason where she is?

There she is! Under the hat.

This hat doesn't belong at a fire station. Jason thinks he knows who it belongs to. What type of job do you think the person has who owns this hat?

The hat belongs to the baker, and she is glad to have it back. She is having a rough day. First, she lost her hat. Then, her cookies, pies, and cakes got all mixed up. Now, she can't remember which things go together. Can you help her sort them into groups of cookies, pies, and cakes?

That looks so much better, and everything looks delicious!

As a reward, the baker tells Jason that he can have any cookie in the display case. These cookies are made in three different shapes. What shapes are they? What shape do you think Jason will pick?

Jason has a hard time deciding, but he finally picks
the yummy cookie that is shaped like a star. Bobo
gets a special doggy biscuit shaped like a bone!

The baker tells Jason there's a fair in town. Jason wants to go! She gives him a map that shows where it is. How many blocks do you think Jason and Bobo will have to walk to get to the fair?

Jason and Bobo have to walk four blocks—two blocks on Main Street and then two blocks on Third Street. Two plus two is four. They're on their way!

Jason loves to play games and win prizes at the
fair. He just put enough balls through the basket
to win the biggest prize! How many baskets do
you think he made? Which prize is the biggest?

Jason made four baskets and won the biggest prize—a big blue bear! Now Jason wants to see if he can win a goldfish.

If Jason gets a ping-pong ball into a fish bowl, he will win all the fish in that bowl. He wants to throw his ball into the bowl with the most fish. Bobo thinks he should throw it into the bowl with the least fish. Which one does Jason want to aim for? Which one does Bobo want him to aim for?

Jason threw his ping-pong ball into the bowl
with three fish. That's the most fish in any of the
bowls. Now he has three new pets to take home.

Speaking of home . . .

Jason wonders what time it is. He thinks it might be time to leave. Can you help him find two clocks in this picture? Here's a hint: one is up high and one is down low.

One clock is up high—above the merry-go-round.
The other clock is down low—at the bottom of
the rocket.

Can you read the time on the clock below the rocket ride? Do you think both clocks show the same time?

Both clocks show the same time: five o'clock. It's time to head home.

Bobo is ready to go, but Jason wants to go on one ride first. He's looking for the ride with the shortest line. Which one is it? Which line is the longest? How many people are in each line?

The merry-go-round has six people in line. The parachute ride has the shortest line—only two people. Jason joins them and now there are three —and Bobo makes four (but I don't think they will let him on the ride)!

When Jason and Bobo finally arrive home, Mom asks Jason to set the table for dinner. He remembers that the spoons go on the right side of the plate and the forks go on the left, but he isn't sure where the right side of the plate is. Can you help?

That looks right. The table is set and Jason is ready to eat. So is Bobo!

After dinner, Jason realizes how tired he is from his busy day. In fact, he's so tired that he has forgotten the right order to do things to get ready for bed. Which picture do you think shows what he would usually do first? Which one would he do second? Which would he do last?

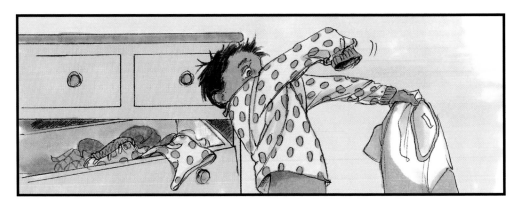

That looks right! Now Jason and Bobo can get a good night's sleep and be ready for another fun day tomorrow.

Good night, Jason and Bobo!

If you liked *Jason and Bobo*, here are a few more
We Both Read books you are sure to enjoy.

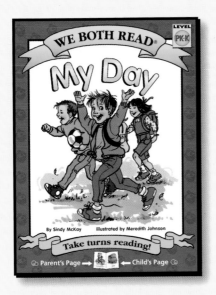

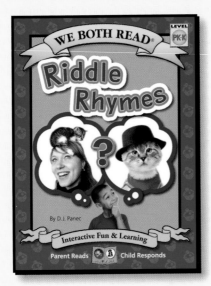

To see all the We Both Read books that are available,
just go to **WeBothRead.com**.